Y045495

Teach Your Dog

FRENCH

D1639346

Funny & surprisingly clever books. Love. Love.
DAWN FRENCH, ACTOR & COMEDIAN

Anne Cakebread not only has the best
name in the Universe, she has also come
up with a brilliantly fun book which will help
humans and canines learn new languages.
RICHARD HERRING, COMEDIAN

People are crackers, mate. They think you can
teach dogs French, when we all know they only
speak Spanish.
ARTHUR SMITH, WRITER & COMEDIAN

Teach Your Dog

FRENCH

Anne Cakebread

Thank you to:
Helen, Marcie, Lily and Nina,
my family, friends and neighbours in
St Dogmaels for all their support and
encouragement, Carolyn at Y Lolfa, and
Maria Woolnough, Pierrette Breuillot and
Charlène Bourg for French translations and
pronunciations.
Merci.

In memory of Frieda, who started us on
the *Teach Your Dog* journey.

First impression 2021

© Anne Cakebread & Y Lolfa Cyf., 2021
This book is subject to copyright and may not be reproduced by any
means except for review purposes without the prior written consent of
the publishers.

Illustrations and design by Anne Cakebread

ISBN: 978-1-80099-032-6
Published and printed in Wales on paper from well-maintained
forests by Y Lolfa Cyf., Talybont, Ceredigion, SY24 5HE Wales
e-mail ylolfa@ylolfa.com
website www.ylolfa.com
tel +44 1970 832 304
fax +44 1970 832 782

I grew up only speaking English.
When I moved to west Wales, I adopted Frieda,
a rescue whippet, who would only obey
Welsh commands.
Slowly, whilst dealing with Frieda, I realised that I was
overcoming my nerves about speaking Welsh aloud,
and my Welsh was improving as a result
– this gave me the idea of creating a series of books
to help others learn.
You don't even have to go to abroad to practise.
If you haven't got a dog, any pet or soft toy will do:
just have fun learning and speaking a new language.

– Anne Cakebread

Teach
Your Dog
French

"Hello"

"Bonjour"

pron:
"Bon-<u>zh</u>o<u>r</u>"

'zh'
as in
'<u>Zh</u>ivago'

soft 'r'
from the
throat

"Come here!"

"Viens ici !"

pron:
"Vee-ya<u>n</u> ee-see!"

almost silent 'n'

“Stop!”

“Arrête-toi !”

pron:

“Arret-twa!”

soft ‘r’ from the throat

‘e’ as in ‘met’

‘a’ as in ‘are’, but shorter

"Do you want
a cuddle?"

**"Tu veux
une caresse ?"**

pron:
"Too vuh oon caress?"

'uh'
as in
'huh'

'oon'
as in
'soon'

soft 'r'
from the
throat

"Catch!"

"Attrape !"

pron:

"**A**-t**r**ap!"

'A'
as in
'm**a**n'

soft 'r'
from the
throat

"Fetch!"

"Rapporte !"

pron:

"Ra-port!"

soft 'r'
from the
throat

'a'
as in
'man'

"Leave it!"

"Laisse ça !"

pron:
Less s<u>a</u>!

'a'
as in
'm<u>a</u>n'

"Sit!"

"Assis !"

pron:

"A-see!"

'A'
as in
'man'

"No!"

"Non !"

pron:
"No**ng**!"

'ong'
as in
's**ong**'

"Stay!"

"Reste !"

pron:
"<u>R</u>est!"

soft 'r'
from the
throat

"Bathtime!"

"Au bain !"

pron:
"Oh ba*n*!"

almost
silent
'n'

"Bedtime!"

"Au lit !"

pron:
"Oh lee!"

"Eat!"

"Mange !"

pron:
"Monzh!"

'zh'
as in
'Zhivago'

"Are you full?".

"Tu n'as plus faim ?"

pron:

"Too n**a** ploo **fam**?"

'a' as in 'm**a**n'

stress this

almost silent 'm'

"All gone"

"C'est fini"

pron:
"Say fin-ee"

"Wake up!"

"Réveille-toi !"

pron:

"<u>R</u>evay-tw<u>a</u>!"

soft 'r' from the throat

'a' as in '<u>a</u>re', but shorter

"Goodnight"

"Bonne nuit"

pron:
"Bon nwee"

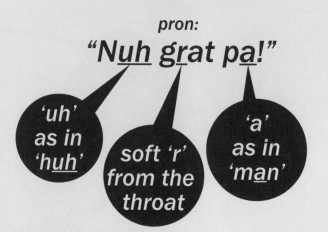

"Don't scratch!"

"Ne gratte pas !"

pron:

"Nuh grat pa!"

'uh' as in 'huh'

soft 'r' from the throat

'a' as in 'man'

"Let's go..."

"On y va..."

pron:
"On ee va..."

'a'
as in
'man'

"Go down!"

"Descends !"

pron:
"Day-song!"

"Up you go!"

"Monte !"

pron:
"Mont!"

"Go straight ahead!"

"Va tout droit !"

pron:
"V**a** too d**r**w**a**!"

'a' as in 'm**a**n'

soft 'r' from the throat

'a' as in '**a**re', but shorter

"Go left!"

"Va à gauche !"

pron:

"Va a go-sh!"

'a'
as in
'man'

'go'
as in
'go', but
shorter

"Turn left!"

"Tourne à gauche !"

pron:

"T__oo__rn __a__ g__o__-sh!"

'oo' as in 's__oo__n'

'a' as in 'm__a__n'

'go' as in '__go__', but shorter

"Turn right!"

"Tourne à droite !"

pron:
"Toorn a drwat!"

'oo' as in 'soon'

'a' as in 'man'

soft 'r' from the throat

"How's it going?"

"Ça va ?"

pron:

"Sa va?"

'a'
as in
'man'

"Do you want to play?"

"Tu veux jouer ?"

pron:

"Too v<u>uh</u> <u>zh</u>oo-way?"

'uh' as in 'h<u>uh</u>'

'zh' as in '<u>Zh</u>ivago'

"Lie down!"

"Couché !"

pron:
"Koo-<u>shay</u>!"

stress
this

"Say 'please'!"

"Dis 's'il te plaît' !"

pron:

"Dee 'seal t<u>uh</u> pl<u>e</u>'!"

'<u>uh</u>' as in 'h<u>uh</u>'

'<u>e</u>' as in 'm<u>e</u>t'

"Can I have a croissant?"

"Je peux avoir un croissant ?"

'Zh' as in '<u>Zh</u>ivago'

'a' as in '<u>a</u>re', but shorter

pron:

"<u>Zh</u>uh puh <u>a</u>vw<u>a</u>-r an cw<u>a</u>-song?"

'a' as in 'm<u>a</u>n'

soft 'r' from the throat

"Very clever"

"Très malin"

pron:
"Tray mal-ann"

soft 'r'
from the
throat

almost
silent
'n'

"It's warm"

"Il fait chaud"

pron:
"Eel fay show"

"It's cold"

"Il fait froid"

pron:
"Eel fay fr̲wa̲"

soft 'r'
from the
throat

'a'
as in
'a̲re', but
shorter

"The weather is nice"

"Il fait beau"

pron:
"Eel fay b<u>ow</u>"

'ow'
as in
'sh<u>ow</u>', but
shorter

"It's raining"

"Il pleut"

pron:
*"Eel plu**h**"*

'uh'
as in
'h**uh**'

"Are you happy?"

"Tu es content 🚹 / contente 🚺?"

pron:

"Too ay con-tong 🚹 / contont 🚺?"

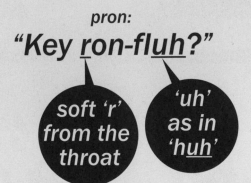

"Have you got enough room?"

"Tu as assez de place ?"

stress this

pron:

"Too a ass-e duh plass?"

'a' as in 'man'

'e' as in 'met'

'uh' as in 'huh'

'a' as in 'man'

"See you soon"

"À bientôt"

pron:

"A bee-an-toe"

'A'
as in
'man'

almost
silent
'n'

"Be quiet!"

"Tais-toi !"

pron:

"Te twa!"

'e'
as in
'met'

'a'
as in
'are', but
shorter

"Who did that?"

"Qui a fait ça ?"

pron:

"Key a fay sa?"

'a'
as in
'man'

"There's a queue
for the loo"

"Il y a la queue
pour les toilettes"

pron:

"Eeleeya la kuh
poor lay twa-let"

soft 'r'
from the
throat

'a'
as in
'man'

5
"cinq"
pron:
"sank"

6
"six"
pron:
"see-ss"

7

"sept"

pron:
"set"

8

"huit"

pron:
"wheat"

9

"neuf"

pron:
"nerf"

10
"dix"
pron:
"dee-ss"

"Thank you"

"Merci"

pron:
"Mare-sea"

soft 'r'
from the
throat

"Merry Christmas"

"Joyeux
Noël"

pron:
"Zhwa-yuh no-el"

'Zh'
as in
'Zhivago'

'uh'
as in
'huh'

"Congratulations!"

"Félicitations !"

pron:
"Fell-ee-see-tass-yo<u>n</u>!"

almost
silent
'n'

"Happy Birthday"

"Bon Anniversaire"

pron:
"Bon Annie-v<u>air</u>-s<u>air</u>"

like
the word
'air'

"I love you"

"Je t'aime"

pron:

"<u>Zh</u>uh tem"

'<u>Zh</u>'
as in
'<u>Zh</u>ivago'

'uh'
as in
'h<u>uh</u>'

"Goodbye"

"Au revoir"

pron:

"Oh ruv-wa-r"

'a'
as in
'are', but
shorter

soft
'r'
from the
throat

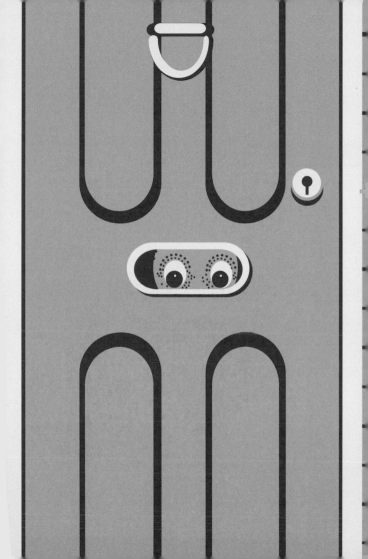

Other titles in this series include:

Teach Your Dog Welsh
Teach Your Cat Welsh
Teach your Dog Irish
Teach Your Dog Cornish
Teach Your Dog Gaelic
Teach Your Cat Manx
Teach Your Dog Spanish
Teach Your Dog Māori
Teach Your Dog Korean
Teach Your Dog Japanese
(Rugby World Cup 2019 Travel Edition)